DR. BOB'S
AMAZING WORLD OF
ANIMALS
RING-TAILED LEMURS

By Ruth Owen

WINDMILL
BOOKS
New York

Published in 2014 by Windmill Books, An Imprint of Rosen Publishing
29 East 21st Street, New York, NY 10010

Editor for Ruby Tuesday Books Ltd: Mark J. Sachner
US Editor: Joshua Shadowens
Designer: Trudi Webb

Photo Credits: Cover, 1, 4–5, 7, 8–9, 10–11, 12–13, 14–15, 16, 18–19, 20–21, 23, 24–25, 26–27, 29, 30
© Shutterstock; 17 © FLPA; 22 © Warren Photographic; 28 © Wikipedia, Public Domain.

Library of Congress Cataloging-in-Publication Data

Owen, Ruth, 1967–
 Ring-tailed lemurs / by Ruth Owen.
    pages cm. — (Dr. Bob's amazing world of animals)
 Includes index.
 ISBN 978-1-47779-040-3 (library) — ISBN 978-1-47779-041-0 (pbk.) —
 ISBN 978-1-47779-042-7 (6-pack)
 1. Ring-tailed lemur—Juvenile literature. I. Title.
 QL737.P95O94 2014
 599.8'3—dc23

                          2013029221

Manufactured in the United States of America

CPSIA Compliance Information: Batch #BW14WM: For Further Information contact Windmill Books, New York, New York at 1-866-478-0556

Contents

The Ring-Tailed Lemur

Welcome to my amazing world of animals. Today, we are visiting the large island country of Madagascar to find out about ring-tailed lemurs.

A ring-tailed lemur

Let's investigate...

Hank's
WOOF OF WISDOM!

Ring-tailed lemurs belong to an animal group called **primates**. They are distant cousins to monkeys, apes, and even humans!

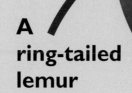

4

There are many different types of lemurs.
They all come from the island of Madagascar.

Ringed, furry tail

Ring-tailed lemurs are named for their super-long tails, which have rings of black and white fur.

The Land of the Lemur

Many ring-tailed lemurs live in zoos around the world. These animals only live wild, though, in one place, Madagascar and the small islands that surround the country.

Madagascar is a large island near Africa. It is in the Indian Ocean.

The red areas on the map are where ring-tailed lemurs can be found.

Ring-tailed lemurs live in hot, dry forests. They also live in places where there are lots of small trees, thick bushes, and other plants.

These lemurs spend about half of their time in the trees and half on the ground.

Ring-Tailed Lemur Bodies

Ring-tailed lemurs have thick gray and white fur. They look a little like a dog mixed with a cat and a raccoon!

A ring-tailed lemur's back legs are longer than its front legs. When it walks on all fours, its bottom sticks up in the air.

When lemurs climb in trees, they use their hands and feet to hold onto branches.

Thick fur

Hands and feet that can grip

Long back legs

Ring-Tailed Lemur Size Chart

Weight adult males and females = up to 6 pounds (2.7 kg)

Hank's WOOF OF WISDOM!

Ring-tailed lemurs have black skin on the palms of their hands and soles of their feet. Their hands and feet also have human-like nails.

An adult ring-tailed lemur's head and body are about 18 inches (46 cm) long.

A ring-tailed lemur's hand

The Girls Are in Charge

Ring-tailed lemurs live in groups called troops. A small troop may have just 6 members, but most troops include 20 to 25 lemurs.

A ring-tailed lemur troop is mostly made up of adult females, their babies, and young lemurs. Some females in the group are more **dominant** than others.

Adult male lemurs follow the troop and hang out with the group, but it's the females who are in charge.

A troop's female members choose where to eat and sleep.

When the troop finds some tasty food, the females get to eat first. The males must wait their turn!

A Lemur Troop's Neighborhood

A ring-tailed lemur troop chooses an area to be its **territory**. The group's territory is where the animals live and find their food.

If a troop finds another group in its territory, the female lemurs act **aggressively** toward the trespassers.

Ring-tailed lemurs don't attack as a group. Each female fights her own battles by leaping or making short, darting runs at another lemur on the other side.

Male lemurs sometimes help the females in a territory war. Usually, however, they wait behind the females for the trouble to be over!

Smelly Messages

Ring-tailed lemurs use scent, or smells, to send messages to other ring-tailed lemurs.

Scent gland

Ring-tailed lemurs produce scent from glands, special body parts, on their bottoms. They also have scent glands on their wrists.

Male ring-tailed lemurs have scent glands on their chests, too.

Ring-tailed lemurs wipe scent onto trees and other objects on the edges of their territory. These smelly messages tell other lemur troops, "This territory is taken!"

Just smelling my messages!

Ring-tailed lemurs also use their urine to mark the edges of their home neighborhood.

Talking Tails

Unlike some of their monkey cousins, ring-tailed lemurs can't hold onto tree branches with their tails. They do use their tails a little like flags, however.

FOLLOW ME!

Hank's
WOOF OF WISDOM!

A ring-tailed lemur's black and white tail may be up to 25 inches (64 cm) long.

When a ring-tailed lemur troop is on the move on the ground, the lemurs hold their tails up in the air.

The tails are like striped flags waving through grass or bushes. As the traveling lemurs move, the group stays together by watching for each other's long tails.

A Lemur's Day

In the land of the lemur it can be very cold at night. So, every morning, ring-tailed lemurs warm up by sunbathing.

A sunbathing ring-tailed lemur

After several hours sunbathing, it's time to look for food.

The troop searches for food
on the ground and in trees.

During the
hot afternoon,
lemurs rest and
sleep. Then, it's
time to look for
more food.

Finally, as darkness falls, the lemurs
get settled into two or three trees
where they spend the night.

What's on the Menu?

Ring-tailed lemurs eat plant foods. In fact, their menu can include food from up to 50 different plants.

Ring-tailed lemurs feed on fruit, flowers, and leaves. They also eat tree bark and **sap**, which is a thick liquid that flows through plants.

When they are **foraging** for food in the treetops, ring-tailed lemurs often leap from tree to tree.

Stink Fights!

When the **mating season** comes around, things can get stinky in lemur land. That's because male ring-tailed lemurs have stink fights over females.

A male lemur gets ready to do battle by rubbing his tail on his scent glands.

A male scenting his tail

Once his tail is good and smelly, a male lemur arches his tail over his back. Then he waves the smelly tail at his opponent.

The stinky power battle can go on for an hour.

Take that!

Time after time, each male rubs scent on his tail and waves it at the other. Finally, the most powerful, or stinkiest, male gets the girl!

A New Family

About four and a half months after mating, a female ring-tailed lemur gives birth. She may give birth to a single baby or twins.

Mother lemur

Baby lemur

These lemur twins are drinking milk.

A baby ring-tailed lemur feeds on milk from its mother's body.

A newborn ring-tailed lemur weighs just over 2 ounces (57 g). The tiny baby is able to cling to its mother's fur as soon as it is born.

Baby ring-tailed lemur

By the time a baby lemur is two weeks old, it rides everywhere on its mother's back.

Little Lemurs

Baby ring-tailed lemurs soon start grabbing at branches. By the time they are three weeks old, they are able to climb about in trees.

Learning to climb!

Little lemurs start eating leaves and other plant foods when they are about six weeks old. They still drink milk, however, until they are four to six months old.

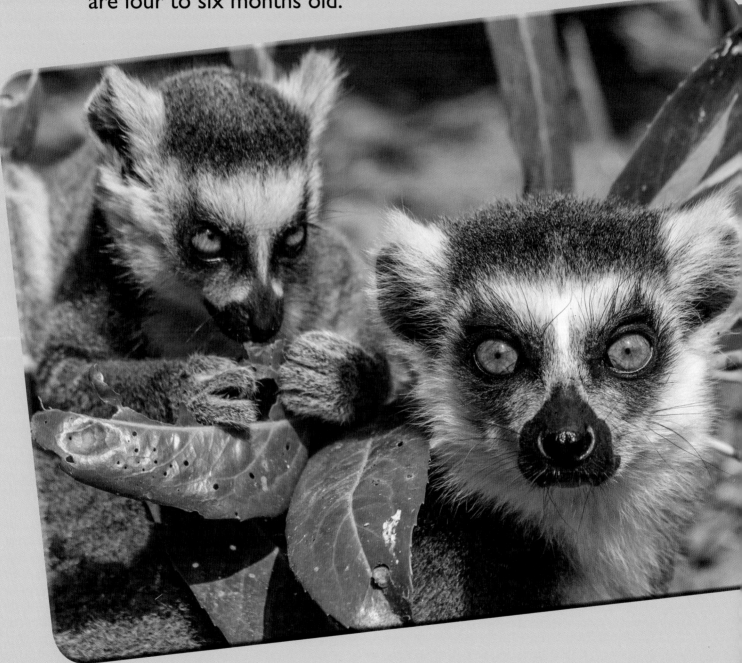

Once they become adults, male ring-tailed lemurs leave their mother's troop and find a new troop. Females stay in the troop where they were born.

The Future for Lemurs

The forests and wild, plant-filled areas of Madagascar are the ring-tailed lemur's home. Sadly, those places are being destroyed by humans.

Hank's
WOOF OF WISDOM!

Trees in Madagascar's forests are cut down for wood and to make space for growing crops.

Thankfully, the government of Madagascar and **conservationists** are working to save Madagascar's forests and wild places.

Areas of land are being protected. In these places, it's now against the law to cut down trees.

If the forests are saved, ring-tailed lemurs and many other types of animals will have a home for the future.

Glossary

aggressively
(uh-GREH-siv-lee)
Ready or likely to attack.

conservationists
(kon-sur-VAY-shun-ists) People who
do work to protect wild animals,
plants, and natural habitats.

dominant (DAH-mih-nunt)
More powerful and important.

foraging (FOR-uj-ing)
Searching for food.

mating season
(MAYT-ing SEE-zun)
A time of year when the males
and females of a particular type of
animal get together to mate and
produce young.

primates (PRY-maytz) Animals
that belong to the group that includes
lemurs, monkeys, apes, and humans.
Primates are mammals. They are
warm-blooded, have backbones
and hair, and feed milk
to their young.

sap (SAP) Liquid that carries water
and nourishment through plants. Sap is
often thick and sticky.

territory (TER-uh-tor-ee) The area
where an animal lives, finds its food,
and finds partners for mating.

Dr. Bob's Fast Fact Board

Ring-tailed lemurs help plants spread their seeds. When lemurs eat a plant's fruit, they also eat the seeds in the fruit. The seeds then pass out of the lemurs in their waste and land on the ground in a new growing place.

Ring-tailed lemurs often leap about in trees that are covered with thorns. Somehow, the lemurs manage to avoid landing on the sharp, painful thorns!

Ring-tailed lemurs rub their fur with foul-smelling juices from millipedes. Scientists think the juices keep insects away and stop the lemurs from being bitten.

Ring-tailed lemurs can live for up to 25 years.

Websites

For web resources related to the subject of this book, go to:

www.windmillbooks.com/weblinks

and select this book's title.

Read More

Baicker, Karen, Kate Delaney, and Sharon Yates. *Lemurs*. Amazing Animals. New York: Gareth Stevens Learning Library, 2009.

Buckingham, Suzanne. *Meet the Ring-Tailed Lemur*. Scales and Tails. New York: PowerKids Press, 2008.

Ganeri, Anita. *Lemur*. A Day In the Life: Rain Forest Animals. Mankato, MN: Capstone Press, 2011.

Index